Personal Financial Planner

to accompany

PERSONAL FINANCE

Skills for Life

VICKIE BAJTELSMIT

Colorado State University

WILEY

John Wiley & Sons, Inc.

ASSOCIATE PUBLISHER	Judith R. Joseph
SENIOR DEVELOPMENT EDITOR	Marian D. Provenzano
SENIOR PRODUCTION EDITOR	William A. Murray
MARKETING MANAGER	Heather King
EDITORIAL ASSISTANT	Masha Maizel
DESIGN DIRECTOR	Harry Nolan
INTERIOR DESIGN	Trisha McFadden
COVER PHOTO	Randy Wells/Corbis Images

This book was set in Avenir Book by GGS Book Services, Atlantic Highlands and printed and bound by Donnelley/Willard. The cover was printed by Phoenix Color.

This book is printed on acid free paper. ∞

To order books or for customer service please, call 1-800-CALL WILEY (225-5945).

ISBN 0-471-70349-4

Printed in the United States of America.

10 9 8 7 6 5 4 3 2 1

The *Personal Financial Planner* is included as a free supplement to *Personal Finance: Skills for Life*. This workbook and its companion interactive worksheets on the text website will make it easier to apply the skills you learn in your personal finance course to developing your own comprehensive financial plan.

Throughout the text, you will see margin references to the relevant *Personal Financial Planner* worksheets, by worksheet number and title. In addition, many of the *Developing Personal Financial Skills for Life* exercises will direct you to one or more of the 55 worksheets included in this workbook. If you complete the worksheets as you go, you'll have a good start on your financial plan by the end of the course.

The *Planner* is produced in a three-hole punch format so that you can easily compile the worksheets that are applicable to your life circumstances. Since many aspects of your financial plan will change over time, you may find it useful to make copies of worksheets that will need to be updated regularly (such as the Personal Cash Flow Statement and Personal Balance Sheet). Alternatively, you can access and download them from the text website. For your convenience, this workbook also includes reference appendices covering time value of money calculations and how to use a financial calculator. The worksheets are in the same order as they appear in the text.

PERSONAL FINANCIAL PLANNER contents

PERSONAL FINANCIAL PLANNER contents

PERSONAL FINANCIAL PLANNER [contents]

Date Recorded:_____

	YOU	YOUR SPOUSE
Full Name:		
Address:		

Phone numbers:
  Home:
  Work:
  Cell:		

E-mail address:		
Date of birth:		
Social Security number:		

Employer:
  Address:
 	
  Phone:		

Driver's license number:		

Dependent 1:
  Name:
  Date of birth:
  Social Security number:		

Dependent 2:
  Name:
  Date of birth:
  Social Security number:		

Dependent 3:
  Name:
  Date of birth:
  Social Security number:		

Dependent 4:
  Name:
  Date of birth:
  Social Security number:		

	YOU	YOUR SPOURSE

Insurance Agent(s):
  Name:
  Company/Address:
  Phone:		

Name: Company/Address: Phone:		

Attorney(s)
  Name:
  Company/Address:
  Phone:
  Name:
  Company/Address:
  Phone:		

Checking:
  Account number:
  Financial institution:
  Website:		

Savings:
  Account number:
  Financial institution:
  Website:		

WORKSHEET 2 | talk about money with your family

<u>Directions:</u> Have several members of your family fill out copies of this worksheet and then compare answers.

1. If you received $2,000 tax-free, what would you do with it?

   $_____ for_____ $_____ for_____

   $_____ for_____ $_____ for_____

2. If you had to make a major reduction in your spending, what would you cut first?

   _____

3. Rank the following activities from 1 to 7, with 1 being the one you would enjoy doing the most and 7 being the one you would enjoy the least:

   _____ Family activities at home   _____ Enjoying some quiet time to myself

   _____ Going out to eat   _____ Participating in my hobby

   _____ Exercising or outdoor recreation   _____ Shopping

   _____ Spending time with friends

4. Indicate whether you agree (A) or disagree (D) with each of the following statements:

   _____ I spend too much money.

   _____ Other members of my family spend too much money.

   _____ Equality in family decision making is important to me.

   _____ I feel good about the way financial decisions are made in my family.

   _____ I believe in enjoying today and letting tomorrow worry about itself.

   _____ I always wish I had more money than I do.

5. I'd like to see our family spend less money on _____ and see more money go for_____.

6. What money problem is the most frequent cause of argument in your family?

   _____

7. What was the most sensible financial action you have taken in your family?

   _____

8. What was the most foolish financial thing you have done in your family?

   _____

9. Do you know the dollar amounts that go in the following blanks?

   Family take-home income is $ _____ per month.

   Family monthly rent or mortgage payment is $ _____ per month.

   Our family spends $ _____ on food each month.

10. Buying on credit is _____

Directions: For each of the following statements, write the number that shows the extent to which the statement accurately describes your views (5 = strongly agree; 4 = agree; 3 = undecided; 2 = disagree; 1 = strongly disagree). Ask members of your family to complete this assessment separately and compare your scores.

_____ **1.** I would be a lot happier if I had more money.

_____ **2.** I usually buy things after they are marked down, and it bothers me when I discover an item I just purchased on sale for less somewhere else.

_____ **3.** I love it when I get a small windfall of money, like a tax refund or birthday gift, so I can spend it on something I usually don't have the money for.

_____ **4.** Whenever possible, I use coupons at the grocery store, and I always look through the newspaper ads to find the best deals on the items I buy regularly.

_____ **5.** If I see something that I want to buy, and I have the money at the moment, I usually go ahead and buy it rather than waiting to get it for a birthday or Christmas present.

_____ **6.** Whenever I make a major purchase, I always feel guilty that I didn't save the money instead.

_____ **7.** It would be worth it to me to pay a little more for brand name clothing since the right clothes are important to how people perceive me at work and school.

_____ **8.** I argue or complain about the cost of things.

_____ **9.** I like to buy nice things for other people at the holidays, even if it means I go over my budget a bit—my friends and family are worth it.

_____**10.** I worry about my finances.

Scoring:

This assessment tells you the degree to which money is a controlling factor in your life. The odd-numbered questions relate to the degree to which you are focused on what money can buy. The even-numbered questions relate to the degree that money adds stress and worry to your life.

Total your scores for each group of questions.

Total for odds: #1, #3, #5, #7, #9 _____

Total for evens: #2, #4, #6, #8, #10 _____

Overall total _____

Your total for the odd-numbered questions can range from 5 to 25. If you score on the low end of this scale, money and the things it can buy are less important to you. If your score is between 20 and 25, you have a tendency to value material possessions and you have difficulty delaying the gratification you get from spending money. Your total for the even-numbered questions can also range from 5 to 25. If your total is 20 to 25, money and financial matters are significant stress producers for you. If your total score is between 40 and 50, money is a controlling factor in your life and you have some unhealthy money habits that will make it more difficult to achieve your financial goals.

[WORKSHEET 4] checklist for interviewing a financial planner

Directions: Make a copy of this worksheet for each prospective planner and use it as an outline for your initial interview.

Name of planner: _____

Company: _____

Address: _____

Phone: _____ Fax: _____

1. How long have you been offering financial planning advice to clients?

☐ Less than 1 year   ☐ 5 to 10 years

☐ 1 to 4 years   ☐ More than 10 years

2. How many clients do you currently have?

☐ Less than 10   ☐ 40 to 79

☐ 10 to 39   ☐ 80 +

3. Briefly describe your work history

4. What educational background qualifies you to be a financial planner?

☐ Certificate   ☐ Advanced degree

☐ Undergraduate degree   ☐ Other _____

5. What financial planning certifications do you have?

☐ Certified Financial Planner™   ☐ Attorney

☐ Certified Public Accountant   ☐ Other

☐ Chartered Financial Consultant

6. What licenses do you hold?

7. Are you or your firm a licensed or registered investment advisor in this state?

8. In which areas do you have experience, and do you specialize in one or more of these areas?

☐ Retirement planning   ☐ Estate planning

☐ Investment planning   ☐ Insurance planning

☐ Tax planning   ☐ Integrated planning

9. What services do you offer?

10. What is your approach to financial planning?

11. How are you paid for your services?

☐ Fee   ☐ Salary

☐ Commission   ☐ Other

12. What do you typically charge?

Hourly rate _____   Flat fee _____

_____ % of assets under management   _____ % commission on annuities

_____ % commission on stocks and bonds   _____ % commission on insurance

_____ % commission on mutual funds

13. Do you have a business affiliation with any company whose products or services you are recommending? If so, explain.

14. Do you provide a written client engagement agreement? If not, why?

Financial Record General Category	Specific Items Within Category	Filed	Lockbox	Safe Deposit
Auto	Insurance policy			
	Title information			
	Repairs/expenses			
	Auto loan/lease information			
Bank	Checking statements and records			
	Savings statements and records			
Credit	Records for each loan or credit account			
	Credit reports			
	Applications for credit			
Home	Mortgage documents and records			
	Homeowner's insurance			
	Receipts for repairs/capital improvements			
	Rental contracts			
Children	Report cards			
	School photos			
	School policies/procedures manual			
	Records of child-care expenses			
	Birth/adoption certificates			
Life/estate	Life insurance policies			
	Billing records			
	Copy of wills			
	Copy of estate plan			
Medical	Billing and insurance records			
	Prescription drug records			
	Health insurance policy			
	Health/immunization records			
Employee benefits	Periodic reports from retirement plans			
	Employer information			
	Other insurance and benefits			
Taxes	Tax statements from employer(s)			
	Tax statements from investments and loans			
	Tax returns			
	Receipts for next tax year			
Budget and bills	Current bills payable			
	Bill receipts			
	Budget records			
Investments	Records of purchases and sales			
	Account activity statements			

[WORKSHEET 6] personal balance sheet

Directions:
1. List the current values of your assets and your debts.
2. Compute Net worth = Total assets − Total debts
   = _____

Assets		**Debts**	
Checking accounts	$ _____	Current bills	
Savings accounts	_____	1. _____	$ _____
Money market accounts	_____	2. _____	_____
U.S. savings bonds	_____	3. _____	_____
Cash value of life insurance	_____	**Total current bills**	_____
Other short-term investments	_____		
Total liquid assets	_____	Credit card balances (list)	
Cars	_____	1. _____	_____
Home furnishings	_____	2. _____	_____
Jewelry/art/collectibles	_____	3. _____	_____
Clothing/personal assets	_____	Alimony/child support owed	_____
Total personal property	_____	Taxes owed (above with-holding)	_____
Market value of investments (stocks, bonds, mutual funds)	_____	Personal loans	_____
Employer retirement plan(s)	_____	Car loans	_____
Individual retirement account(s)	_____	**Total short-term debts**	_____
Other retirement savings	_____	Home mortgage balance	_____
College savings plan	_____	Home equity loans	_____
Other savings plans	_____	Other real estate loans	_____
Total investment assets	_____	Students loans	_____
Market value of home	_____	Other investment loans	_____
Market value of investment real estate	_____	Other liabilities/debts	_____
Total real property	_____	**Total long-term debts**	_____
Total assets	_____	**Total debts**	_____

[WORKSHEET 7] personal cash flow statement

Directions:
1. List all your cash inflows and outflows.
2. Compute Net cash flow = Total cash inflows − Total cash outflows
= _____

Cash Inflows			Cash Outflows		
	Monthly	January 1 to December 31		Monthly	January 1 to December 31
Salary/wage income (gross)	_____	_____	Income and payroll taxes	_____	_____
Interest/dividend Income	_____	_____	Groceries		
			Housing		
Other income (self-employment)	_____	_____	Mortgage or rent	_____	_____
Rental income (after expenses)	_____	_____	Property tax	_____	_____
			Insurance	_____	_____
Cash from sale of assets	_____	_____	Maintenance/ repairs	_____	_____
Student loans	_____	_____	Utilities		
			Heating	_____	_____
			Electric	_____	_____
Scholarships	_____	_____	Water and sewer		
Other income	_____	_____	Cable/phone/ satellite	_____	_____
Gifts	_____	_____	Car loan payments	_____	_____
Total Cash Inflows	_____	_____	Car maintenance/ gas	_____	_____
			Credit card payments	_____	_____
			Other loan payments	_____	_____
			Other taxes	_____	_____
			Insurance		
			Life	_____	_____
			Health	_____	_____
			Auto	_____	_____
			Disability	_____	_____
			Other insurance	_____	_____
			Clothing	_____	_____
			Gifts	_____	_____
			Other consumer goods	_____	_____
			Child-care expenses	_____	_____
			Sports-related expenses	_____	_____

Health club dues	_____	_____
Uninsured medical expenses	_____	_____
Education	_____	_____
Vacations and travel	_____	_____
Entertainment	_____	_____
Alimony/child support	_____	_____
Charitable contributions	_____	_____
Required pension contributions	_____	_____
Magazine subscriptions/books	_____	_____
Other payments/ expenses	_____	_____
Total cash outflows	_____	_____

[WORKSHEET 8] spending log

Directions: Copy this worksheet and use it to keep careful track of all your expenditures for one or more weeks.

Monday Description	$	Tuesday Description	$	Wednesday Description	$

Thursday Description	$	Friday Description	$	Saturday/Sunday Description	$

[WORKSHEET 9] personal financial ratios

<u>Directions:</u> Use your personal financial statements to calculate your personal financial ratios. Record them on this worksheet, critically evaluate your current financial situation, identify areas to work on, and reevaluate periodically to track your progress.

Personal Financial Criteria	__/__/__	__/__/__	__/__/__
Net worth			
Net cash flow			
Liquidity ratio $= \dfrac{\text{Liquid assets}}{\text{Monthly expenses}}$			
Debt ratio $= \dfrac{\text{Total debt}}{\text{Total assets}}$			
Debt payment ratio $= \dfrac{\text{Total monthly debt payments}}{\text{After-tax monthly income}}$			
Mortgage debt service ratio $= \dfrac{\text{Monthly mortgage debt service}}{\text{Gross monthly income}}$			
Savings ratio $= \dfrac{\text{Monthly savings}}{\text{After-tax income}}$			
Overall evaluation of current finances:			
Specific areas that I need to work on:			

WORKSHEET 10 · prioritizing goals

Directions: Since you can't necessarily work on achieving all your financial goals at once, you need to prioritize them. This worksheet will help you think about which of your goals should have greater priority right now.

Short-Term Goals	Priority	Estimated Cost	Long-Term Goals	Priority	Estimated Cost
Vacation	1 2 3	$_____	Reduce credit	1 2 3	$_____
New car	1 2 3	$_____	Change jobs	1 2 3	$_____
House repair	1 2 3	$_____	College fund	1 2 3	$_____
Car repair	1 2 3	$_____	Remodel house	1 2 3	$_____
Eat out more often	1 2 3	$_____	New house	1 2 3	$_____
Hire a housecleaner	1 2 3	$_____	Go back to school	1 2 3	$_____
Catch up on bills	1 2 3	$_____	Retire comfortably	1 2 3	$_____
Start an IRA	1 2 3	$_____	Die rich	1 2 3	$_____
Buy life insurance	1 2 3	$_____	Other_____	1 2 3	$_____
Other_____	1 2 3	$_____	Other_____	1 2 3	$_____
Other_____	1 2 3	$_____	Other_____	1 2 3	$_____
Total		$_____	**Total**		$_____

Directions: Identify three short-term and three long-term personal financial goals that are of the highest priority to you. Break down these goals into realistic and achievable steps.

SHORT-TERM GOALS

Goal 1_____

a._____

b._____

c._____

d._____

Goal 2_____

a._____

b._____

c._____

d._____

Goal 3_____

a._____

b._____

c._____

d._____

LONG-TERM GOALS

Goal 1_____

a._____

b._____

c._____

d._____

Goal 2_____

a._____

b._____

c._____

d._____

Goal 3_____

a._____

b._____

c._____

d._____

WORKSHEET 12   budget forecast

Directions: Use your current financial information to forecast your income and expenses for next year. In the first pass, simply estimate based on known expenses and inflation. Once you determine your forecast net cash flow, recast your budget in a second pass that includes planned reductions in expenditures and your plan for achieving financial goals.

	Previous Year Actual	Next Year First Pass	Final	Comments
CASH INFLOWS	200__	200__	200__	
After-tax income	_____	_____	_____	
CASH OUTFLOWS				
Groceries and eating out	_____	_____	_____	
Housing	_____	_____	_____	
Mortgage principal and interest	_____	_____	_____	
Repairs and expenses	_____	_____	_____	
Property taxes	_____	_____	_____	
Insurance	_____	_____	_____	
Utilities				
Heating and electric	_____	_____	_____	
Water and sewer	_____	_____	_____	
Cable, phone, and satellite	_____	_____	_____	
Car loan payment(s)	_____	_____	_____	
Car maintenance and gas	_____	_____	_____	
Credit card payments	_____	_____	_____	
	_____	_____	_____	
Insurance				
Life	_____	_____	_____	
Health	_____	_____	_____	
Auto	_____	_____	_____	
Disability	_____	_____	_____	
Clothing	_____	_____	_____	
Gifts	_____	_____	_____	
Other consumer goods	_____	_____	_____	
Child-care expenses	_____	_____	_____	
Sports-related expenses	_____	_____	_____	
Health club dues	_____	_____	_____	
Uninsured medical expense	_____	_____	_____	
Education and training	_____	_____	_____	
College fund	_____	_____	_____	
Vacations	_____	_____	_____	

Entertainment			
Charitable contributions			
IRA contributions			
Magazines and books			
Other expenses			
Total cash outflows			
Net Personal Cash Flow			

Overall evaluation of my household budget:

Specific budgetary objectives for the coming year:

Directions: Compare your budgeted monthly income and expenses to the actual amounts for a period of months and calculate your budget variance (= Budgeted amount − Actual amount).

	Budgeted Monthly	Actual Monthly Income and Expenses					
		__/__/__	Variance	__/__/__	Variance	__/__/__	Variance
CASH INFLOWS							
CASH OUTFLOWS							
Groceries and eating out							
Housing							
Mortgage debt service							
House repairs and expenses							
Utilities							
Heating							
Electric							
Water and sewer							
Cable, phone, and satellite							
Car loan payments							
Car maintenance and gas							
Credit card payments							
Insurance							
Life							
Health							
Auto							
Disability							
Clothing							
Gifts							
Other consumer goods							
Child-care expenses							
Sports-related expenses							
Health club dues							
Uninsured medical expenses							
Education and training							
College fund							
Vacations							
Entertainment							
Charitable contributions							
IRA contributions							
Magazines and books							
Other expenses							
Total cash outflows							
Net Personal Cash Flow							
Cumulative variance							

<u>Directions</u>: Use the following exercise to evaluate your goal orientation. For each of the following statements, write the number that shows the extent to which the statement accurately describes your views (5 = strongly agree; 4 = agree; 3 = undecided; 2 = disagree; 1 = strongly disagree).

_____ **1.** Buying things for myself makes me feel guilty.

_____ **2.** The happiness of my family is more important to me than my career satisfaction.

_____ **3.** Parents are not obligated to leave an inheritance for their children.

_____ **4.** Parents should pay for their children's college education.

_____ **5.** I regularly do volunteer work.

_____ **6.** Before I spend any of my paycheck on extras, I make sure that I have paid my regular bills.

_____ **7.** If I had children, I would want to buy a home in a nice neighborhood near a good school.

_____ **8.** I would not consider a career that required too much travel away from home.

_____ **9.** My favorite type of vacation is to stay at home with my family.

_____ **10.** Every year, I donate clothes, books, or food to a charity.

<u>Scoring:</u>
Total your score for all questions: _____.

<u>Interpretation</u>: A score of 10 to 30 may indicate that you have a greater focus on yourself than others. Your goals might include those that provide more immediate benefit to yourself, such as vacations and consumer goods. A score of 40 to 50 may indicate that your goals are focused on others' needs rather than your own. You should watch out for your tendency to underallocate resources to your future needs, such as retirement and health care.

WORKSHEET 15 informational interview

Directions:
Find out more about career paths by interviewing people in different careers. Ask each person you interview the following:

Interview Questions	1	2	3
1. How did you decide on this career and this employer?			
2. What did you study in college or graduate school that prepared you for this career?			
3. What is a typical workday like?			
4. What is a typical starting salary and benefits package?			
5. What do you like best about your job?			
6. What do you like least about your job?			
7. What is your greatest challenge?			
8. What is your career and salary advancement potential in this career?			
9. What is your best advice to someone who is thinking about this as a career alternative?			
10. Do you have any good sources of information about this career that you could share with me?			
11. Follow-up comments:			

[WORKSHEET 16] personal and employment data

Organize the information you may want to include on your résumé by completing the followingworksheet:

Education (not including high school)

School attended	Location	Degree and Year	G.P.A.	Dates

Honors and Awards

Name of award/scholarship	Explanation	Dates

Employment

Employer	Position	Responsibilities	Dates

Skills (e.g., oral and written communications, leadership, time management, technical, and computer skills, project management, teamwork)

Type of skill	How obtained/learned	Specific example

Extracurricular Activities (including volunteer work)

Organization	Leadership positions	Dates

References

Name	Relationship	Employer	Address	Phone

WORKSHEET 17 | cover letter template

Use this template to help you organize the body of your cover letter. The letter should identify the job you are interested in and why your skills are a good match with the company's needs.

Your name (Use larger font)   _____
Your address   _____
                              _____

Your phone number(s)   _____
Your e-mail address   _____

Name of contact at firm   _____
Address   _____
                              _____

Re: [Identify the purpose of the letter.]

Dear Ms./Mr./Mrs./Dr._____ [Be sure to spell the name correctly and use the correct title.]

[Introduction]
The first paragraph should identify the position you are interested in, the name of someone influential, if appropriate, who recommended that you apply, and make a general statement as to why you would be a good choice for the job (based on education, skills, or experience).

_____
_____
_____
_____
_____
_____

[Body]
The second paragraph should give some more specifics about your skills and how they will fit in with the needs of the company and add value. You should emphasize the characteristics that make you stand out from the rest (including leadership and communication skills).

_____
_____
_____
_____
_____
_____
_____

[Request for contact]
Thank the letter's recipient for considering you, indicate your interest in and availability for an interview, tell him or her how you plan to follow up, and how that individual can contact you.

[WORKSHEET 18] federal income tax estimator

My filing status   _____

Tax form   _____

Income from all sources less exclusions   _____

_____

_____

Total income   = _____

Less adjustments to income   − _____

Adjusted gross income   = _____

Less deductions

Standard deduction   _____

OR

Itemized deductions

    Medical (>7.5 AGI)   _____

    State, local income taxes   _____

    Property taxes   _____

    Mortgage interest   _____

    Charitable contributions   _____

    Casualty and theft losses   _____

    Miscellaneous (>2% AGI)   _____

    Total Itemized   = _____

Less exemptions:

    #___ × Amount_____   = _____

Taxable income   = _____

Estimated tax (based on current tax tables) = _____

Less tax credits   _____

_____

_____

Total taxes owed   = _____

Less estimated taxes and withholding   _____

Tax due or refund   = _____

Strategies for reducing taxes owed for this year or next:

1. _____

2. _____

3. _____

4. _____

	Three Most Popular Tax-Preparation Software Packages		
Product Name	_____	_____	_____
Price			
Includes state tax forms			
Includes electronic filing option			
Interfaces with finance software			
People I know who use it			
Reported consumer ratings			
Includes all forms I need			
Easy to install and use			
Other comparisons			

STEPS:
1. What are your cash management needs?
2. How are you currently meeting those needs?
3. What alternatives should you consider and what services do you still need?

STEP 1: CASH MANAGEMENT NEEDS
a. My liquid assets are sufficient to cover _____ times my monthly expenses.
b. Based on my current balance sheet and cash flow statement, my liquidity ratio is _____.
c. My short-term cash management goals include:

STEP 2: CURRENT STRATEGIES			STEP 3. OTHER ALTERNATIVES
Type of Service	Financial Institution(s)	APY (%)	Type of Service Needed
Transaction needs (Regular or interest-earning checking, debit cards, money orders)			
Savings accounts (Regular savings, CDs, money market accounts, money market mutual funds, US savings bonds)			
Borrowing (Credit cards, overdraft protection, car and personal loans, home mortgages)			
Other services (Special checks, online banking, electronic payments, investment and financial services)			

Part 1: Adjust the Bank Statement

<u>Amount ($)</u>

1. Enter the balance on your current bank statement. _____

2. Add total new deposits. _____
(Include all deposits made that do not appear on bank statement.)

3. Subtract total outstanding checks. _____
(Include all checks written that do not appear on bank statement.)

Adjusted bank balance _____

Part 2: Adjust Your Check Register

1. Enter the balance from your check register. _____

2. Add automatic and ATM deposits not yet recorded. _____

3. Subtract automatic and ATM withdrawals not yet recorded. _____

4. Subtract bank charges. _____
(Monthly fees, minimum balance fees, ATM fees)

5. Add interest earned. _____

Adjusted checkbook register _____

Part 3: Reconcile Bank Statement and Check Register

The adjusted bank balance and the adjusted checkbook register should be equal. If not, then one or more of the following is true:

a. You made a math error.

b. You didn't balance your checkbook last month.

c. You neglected to enter one or more transactions.

d. Your bank made an error.

Directions: Compare alternative financial service providers based on desired features, summarizing the information in the table below.

Make your decision based on the "four P's":

PRODUCTS: Does the financial institution offer the selection of products you need?
Do the products have the features you need?

PRICE: Are the financial products competitively priced?

PEOPLE: Does the financial institution provide the desired level of customer service?

PLACE: Is the financial institution located conveniently for your needs?

Financial Institution Name			
PRODUCTS			
Free checking			
Unlimited checks			
Online account review			
Bill-paying service			
Debit card			
Overdraft protection			
IRAs			
Home equity loans			
PRICE			
Checking account fees			
Checking account interest			
Fee for using other ATM			
Savings account interest			
PEOPLE			
Prompt/courteous service			
Knowledgeable staff			
PLACE			
Convenient			
Sufficient free ATMs			
Online presence			

[WORKSHEET 23] comparing credit cards

Directions: Identify credit card alternatives and compare their features by completing this worksheet.

CREDIT CARD ALTERNATIVES

CREDIT CARD FEATURE				
Annual fee				
APR % on purchases				
APR % on cash advances				
Credit limit				
Grace period				
Frequent flier miles				
Insurance included				
ATM fees				
Rebate in purchases				
Other features				

<u>Directions</u>: For each of the following statements, write the number that shows the extent to which the statement accurately describes your views (5 = strongly agree; 4 = agree; 3 = undecided; 2 = disagree; 1 = strongly disagree).

_____ **1.** I consider how things might be in the future and try to influence current circumstances with my day-to-day behavior.

_____ **2.** I only act to satisfy my immediate concerns, figuring that the future will take care of itself.

_____ **3.** I often engage in a particular behavior in order to achieve outcomes that may not result for many years.

_____ **4.** My behavior is more influenced by things that will happen in the near future (a matter of weeks or days) than it is by events that will likely occur a long time in the future.

_____ **5.** I am willing to sacrifice my immediate happiness or well-being in order to achieve future outcomes.

_____ **6.** I generally ignore warnings about possible future problems because I think the problems will be resolved before they reach crisis level.

_____ **7.** I think it's important to take warnings about negative outcomes seriously even if the negative outcome will not occur for many years.

_____ **8.** Even when I know I should be studying or working on projects that are due later in the semester, I am usually willing to go out and do something fun with my friends instead.

_____ **9.** I think it's more important to focus on actions that have important future consequences than on actions with less important immediate consequences.

_____**10.** I prefer to spend my money on things that I can enjoy right now, rather than saving for a long time to purchase something in the future.

<u>Scoring:</u>
This is an assessment of your tendency toward either immediate gratification or long-term planning, an aspect of your personality that can affect your spending behavior as well as your willingness to incur consumer debt. Add up your total for the even-numbered statements (2, 4, 6, etc.) and your total for the odd-numbered statements (1, 3, 5, etc.). If your total for the odd-numbered statements is greater than your total for the even-numbered statements, then you tend to be more forward-looking and considerate of the future consequences of your actions. You are less likely to spend impulsively and to use credit cards for immediate gratification. If your score for the odd-numbered statements is greater, then the opposite is true—you are inclined to do things today without considering the long-term consequences. Of course, you may find that you exhibit a balance between these two extremes.

Source: Adapted from Lawrence J. Belcher, "Behavior Attitudes Toward Credit and Bankruptcy: Evidence from College Student Surveys," Working Paper, Stetson University, 2003.

Type of Debt	Interest Rate (APR)	Annual Fees	Minimum Payment	Most Recent Finance Charge	Balance Still Owed
Credit cards	_____	_____	_____	_____	_____
	_____	_____	_____	_____	_____
	_____	_____	_____	_____	_____
	_____	_____	_____	_____	_____
Student loans	_____	_____	_____	_____	_____
	_____	_____	_____	_____	_____
	_____	_____	_____	_____	_____
Auto loans	_____	_____	_____	_____	_____
	_____	_____	_____	_____	_____
	_____	_____	_____	_____	_____
Other consumer loans	_____	_____	_____	_____	_____
	_____	_____	_____	_____	_____
	_____	_____	_____	_____	_____
Home equity loans	_____	_____	_____	_____	_____
	_____	_____	_____	_____	_____
	_____	_____	_____	_____	_____
Mortgage loans	_____	_____	_____	_____	_____
	_____	_____	_____	_____	_____
Totals				_____	_____

Directions:
1. Complete a consumer credit application.
2. Using this information, rate yourself on each of the five c's of credit, using the following scale:
   4 = excellent; 3 = good; 2 = needs work; 1 = unacceptable.
3. Based on your assessment, identify goals for improving your creditworthiness.

	Score	Notes:
Capacity Wage, salary, and other income sufficient to make payments Affordable current monthly payment obligations	_____	
Capital Positive net worth, appropriate for life-cycle stage	_____	
Collateral Valuable assets in addition to income (checking, savings, investment accounts) Adequate collateral for loan (if applicable)	_____	
Character Previous experience with credit Past credit history indicates a good attitude toward repaying debts No history of bankruptcy Stable employment and residency	_____	
Conditions Job and employer security General economic conditions favorable	_____	

Plan for improving creditworthiness:

WORKSHEET 27 evaluating credit goals

<u>Directions:</u>
Identify three financial goals that would result in increased borrowing for your household. Evaluate the impact that the probable loan amounts and payments would have on your financial ratios. If you aren't sure how much the payment would be, use Worksheet 28 to calculate it.

Financial Goal #1: _____

Type of loan required   _____
Probable amount of loan _____
Probable loan payment   _____
Impact on financial ratios _____
Other factors to consider _____

Financial Goal #2: _____

Type of loan required   _____
Probable amount of loan _____
Probable loan payment   _____
Impact on financial ratios _____
Other factors to consider _____

Financial Goal #3: _____

Type of loan required   _____
Probable amount of loan _____
Probable loan payment   _____
Impact on financial ratios _____
Other factors to consider _____

Directions:

1. Identify debt obligations that you would like to pay off within a scheduled period of time.

2. Develop a plan for making monthly payments to achieve this goal.

Example: You have a $5,000 student loan, with an APR of 6%. You want to repay it in 10 years.

		Example	Debt #1	Debt #2	Debt #3
Owed to		First National Bank of Omaha			
Balance outstanding	PV	5,000			
Number of periods to repay	N	10 × 12 = 120			
Monthly rate =APR%/12	I	6/12 = 0.5			
Solve for: monthly payment necessary to repay the debt	PMT	$55.51			

Alternative:
Use an equation to solve for the payment. Remember to enter the interest rate in decimal format:

$$PMT = PV \times \frac{i}{\left[1-\left(\frac{1}{1+i}\right)^n\right]} = \frac{PV}{PVIFA_{i,n}}$$

Example: $PMT = \$5,000 \times \frac{0.005}{\left[1-\left(\frac{1}{1.005}\right)^{120}\right]} = \$55.51$

	Date	Lease/ Loan Payment	Fuel	Auto Insurance	Tolls and Parking	Repairs and Maintenance	Registration and License	Monthly Total
January								
February								
March								
April								
May								
June								

	Date	Lease/ Loan Payment	Fuel	Auto Insurance	Tolls and Parking	Repairs and Maintenance	Registration and License	Monthly Total
July								
August								
September								
October								
November								
December								

Before shopping for a car, evaluate your needs and wants.

	Must Have	Would Like
Automatic transmission	☐	☐
All-wheel drive	☐	☐
Dual front airbags	☐	☐
Side curtain airbags	☐	☐
Air conditioning	☐	☐
Antilock brakes	☐	☐
Power seats	☐	☐
Power windows and doors	☐	☐
Sunroof	☐	☐
Upgraded music system	☐	☐
Computer navigation system	☐	☐
Extra-sized gas tank	☐	☐
Split rear seat	☐	☐
Leather interior	☐	☐
Driver seat lumbar adjustment	☐	☐
Third row seats	☐	☐
Cruise control	☐	☐
Other _____	☐	☐
Other _____	☐	☐

WORKSHEET 31 lease versus buy—automobile

Cost of Leasing

Capitalized cost reduction and security deposit _____

Foregone interest on capitalized cost

   reduction and security deposit _____

Total lease payments (= monthly payment $\times$ _____ months) _____

Expected end-of-lease charges _____

Less return of security deposit _____

Total cost of leasing _____

Cost of Buying

Down payment _____

Foregone interest on down payment _____

Total loan payments (= monthly payment $\times$ _____ months) _____

Less expected end-of-loan value _____

Total cost of buying _____

WORKSHEET 32 — lease versus buy—housing

Cost of Renting	**1 year**	**5 years**
Total rent payments (= monthly × 12/year)	_____	_____
Renter's insurance (= $_____/year)	_____	_____
After-tax interest lost on security deposit	_____	_____
(= ___ months rent @ ___% /year)	_____	_____
Total cost of renting	_____	_____

Cost of Buying	**1 year**	**5 years**
Total mortgage payments (= monthly	_____	_____
principal and interest x 12/year)	_____	_____
Property tax	_____	_____
Homeowner's insurance		
Private mortgage insurance	_____	_____
(if < 20% down = 1/2% of mortgage/year)	_____	_____
Repair and maintenance expenses	_____	_____
Down payment	_____	_____
Closing costs	_____	_____
Lost after-tax interest on down payment and		
closing costs @ ___%/year)	_____	_____
Subtotal: costs	_____	_____
Less savings from repaying principal	_____	_____
Less appreciation of home (@___%/year)	_____	_____
Less tax savings from interest deduction	_____	_____
Less tax savings from property tax deduction	_____	_____
Less tax savings from points deduction	_____	_____
Subtotal: savings	_____	_____
Total cost of buying = (costs − savings)	_____	_____

[WORKSHEET 33] calculating affordable home price

STEP 1.
    Monthly amount you can allocate to total housing costs   _____

STEP 2.
    a. Expected cost of property taxes   _____
    b. Expected cost of homeowner's insurance   _____
    c. Expected cost of repairs and maintenance   _____
    d. Expected cost of association dues   _____
    e. Total nonfinancing housing costs (= a + b + c + d)   _____

    Total available for financing costs (principal and interest)
    (= Step 1 − 2e)   _____

STEP 3.
    a. Mortgage factor$_{i,n}$ (Exhibit A-6, 6%, 360 months)   _____
    b. Total available for financing costs (from Step 2)   _____
    c. Maximum affordable mortgage amount (= 3a × 3b)   _____

STEP 4.
    a. Down payment available   _____
    b. Gifts from parents or others   _____
    c. Expected closing costs   _____
    d. Maximum house you can afford (= 3c + 4a + 4b − 4c)   _____

WORKSHEET 34   are you a risk-taker?

<u>Directions</u>: For each of the following questions, indicate whether it is true of your behavior or reflects your opinion: (1) usually, (2) sometimes, or (3) rarely.

_____ **1.** I obey the speed limit.

_____ **2.** I get a regular annual physical every year.

_____ **3.** I brush my teeth and floss every day.

_____ **4.** I never leave my home unlocked when I'm away.

_____ **5.** I always pay my bills on time.

_____ **6.** When I drive in traffic, I make sure that I'm not too close to the car in front of me.

_____ **7.** I don't often pass slow-moving vehicles even if it means I'll be late for work or school.

_____ **8.** I never set off fireworks on the Fourth of July.

_____ **9.** Before I leave my house, I check to be sure that electrical appliances (such as the coffeemaker or iron) are turned off.

_____ **10.** When it snows, I clear my driveway and sidewalks promptly.

_____ **11.** If I had a child, I wouldn't let him or her have a trampoline because it's too dangerous.

_____ **12.** I don't participate in any dangerous sports.

<u>Scoring</u>:
Add up your total points. The higher your score, the more of a risk-taker you are in the nonfinancial aspects of your life.

	Do You Own?	Value?
Real property		
House	☐	_____
Outbuildings	☐	_____
Pool	☐	_____
Driveway	☐	_____
Fence/retaining wall	☐	_____
Personal property		
Clothes	☐	_____
Furniture	☐	_____
Jewelry/watches	☐	_____
Firearms	☐	_____
Dishes/silver/household goods	☐	_____
Artwork/collectibles	☐	_____
Musical instruments	☐	_____
Money/securities	☐	_____
Office equipment	☐	_____
Business inventory and tools	☐	_____
Vehicles and boats	☐	_____
Sports equipment	☐	_____
Others _____	☐	_____

In what areas do I need to consider changes to meet current or future needs?

Homeowner's
Insurance company _____
Agent name _____
Agent address _____
Agent phone _____
Policy number _____
Annual premium _____
Coverage limits _____
Deductibles _____

Automobile
Insurance company _____
Agent name _____
Agent address _____
Agent phone _____
Policy number _____
Annual premium _____
Coverage limits _____
Deductibles _____

Personal umbrella
Insurance company _____
Agent name _____
Agent address _____
Agent phone _____
Policy number _____
Annual premium _____
Coverage limits _____
Deductibles _____

In comparison shopping for property and liability insurance, it's important to provide the same information to each potential insurer so that your quotes will be comparable.

Automobile
Vehicle characteristics (year, make, model)_____
Insured characteristics (age, sex, driving record, full-time or occasional driver)
_____
Potential discounts (good student, driver education)_____

Company Name			

Agent's name
  Address
  Phone			

Policy term (6 or 12 months)			
Total premium			

Liability coverage
  Per person
  Per accident
  Property			

Deductibles
  Collision
  Comprehensive			

Medical payments per person			

Uninsured motorist
  Per person
  Per accident			

Other coverage			
Other factors to consider (e.g., multiple policy discounts, insurer reputation)			

1. Holidays

_____ days per year

_____ paid _____ unpaid

2. Vacation/Personal leave

_____ days per year

_____ paid _____ unpaid

3. Disability coverage

_____ sick days per year

_____ paid _____ unpaid

_____ days short-term disability

_____ day waiting period _____ % of salary paid

_____ days long-term disability

_____ day waiting period _____ % of salary paid

4. Group health insurance

Paid by: _____ Employer _____ Employee _____ Both

Type: _____ Fee-for-service (like Blue Cross Blue Shield)

_____ HMO

_____ PPO or other managed-care plan

_____ Catastrophic

_____ Prescription drug plan

5. Employer-sponsored retirement plans

Type: _____ Defined benefit

_____ 401k or other defined contribution plan

_____ Employee stock ownership plan

_____ Profit-sharing plan

_____ Mandatory participation _____ Optional participation

Contribution by: _____ Employer _____ Employee

6. Life insurance

Type: _____ Term (no cash value) _____ Permanent

Amount: _____

Paid by: _____ Employer _____ Employee _____ Both

7. Dental expense insurance

Paid by: _____ Employer _____ Employee _____ Both

8. Other fringe benefits

Employer Offers		Employer Pays for
_____	Flexible spending account	_____
_____	Child-care facility	_____
_____	Vision/hearing	_____
_____	Other _____	_____

[WORKSHEET 39] health, life, disability, and long-term care insurance inventory

In what areas do I need to consider changes to meet current or future needs?

Health
Insurance company
Agent name
Agent address
Agent phone
Policy number
Annual premium
Coverage limits
Deductibles

Disability Income
Insurance company
Agent name
Agent address
Agent phone
Policy number
Annual premium
Coverage limits
Deductibles

Life Insurance
Insurance company
Agent name
Agent address
Agent phone
Policy number
Annual premium
Coverage limits
Deductibles

Long-Term Care
Insurance company
Agent name
Agent address
Agent phone
Policy number
Annual premium
Coverage limits
Deductibles

Directions:

1. Review your records for the previous calendar year and summarize the health costs incurred by your household.
2. For each cost category, identify whether it was out-of-pocket, partially or fully paid by insurance.
3. Evaluate whether your health insurance is adequate for your current and future needs.

Category of Health Expenditure	Total for Period	Amount Paid out-of-Pocket	Amount Paid by Insurance	Assessment of Insurance Plan to Meet Current/Future Needs
Prescription drugs				
Wellness care (checkups and immunizations)				
Other physician office visits				
Hospital				
Laboratory and diagnostic tests				
Over-the-counter medication				
Surgeons, anesthesia				
Dental and orthodonture				
Vision and hearing				
Medical devices and equipment				
Home health aides				
Nursing or rehabilitation care				
Other health care				

Directions:
Complete this worksheet to estimate your monthly expenses during periods of disability and the resources you currently have in place to meet those expenses. If your resources are insufficient, consider purchasing disability insurance.

Evaluation of Monthly Expenses
1. Enter current household expenses.   _____
2. Subtract any expenses that you would not incur
   (or which could be eliminated from the household
   budget) while you are disabled:
   a. Job-related expenses   _____
   b. Contributions to savings   _____
   c. Unnecessary expenditures   _____
   d. Other   _____

3. Expected expenses when disabled   ══════════════════════

Resources Available to Meet Needs
4. Identify days of replacement income: _____
   a. Number of vacation days   _____
   b. Number of personal days   _____
   c. Number of sick days   _____
   d. Short-term disability   _____
      Waiting period = _____days
      Replaces ____% of predisability income
   Total days before replacement income needed =   _____

5. Identify sources and amounts of after-tax income:
   a. Spouse's income   _____
   b. Income from investments   _____
   c. Social Security disability insurance   _____
   d. Group disability insurance through employer plan   _____
      Waiting period = _____ days
      Replaces ____% of predisability income
   e. Other disability coverage in place   _____
   f. Total income when disabled   ══════════════════════

Additional Disability Coverage Needed
   = Line 4 − Line 5f   ══════════════════════

[WORKSHEET 42] evaluating employment offers

<u>Directions:</u>
1. Enter wage, salary, and fringe benefit information for the job offers you are considering in the table below. (Make additional copies of the worksheet as necessary.)
2. Compare each element of job compensation in the highest cost area.
3. Calculate the net difference in compensation.

	Job #1	Job #2	#1−#2
Cost of living index	$Index_H$ =	$Index_{L(2)}$ =	
Unadjusted salary			
Adjusted salary = Equivalent high-cost salary		$= \dfrac{Index_H \times Salary}{Index_L}$	
Health premiums paid by employer			
Life insurance paid by employer			
Total paid personal, sick, and vacation days			
Adjusted value of paid days		Value per day = $\dfrac{Adjusted\ salary}{Days\ worked\ per\ year}$	= Difference in days × Value/day
Employer contributions to retirement savings			
Value of other retirement plans			
Value of other fringe benefits			
Net difference			

Directions:
1. Identify a financial goal (from Worksheet 10).
2. Complete this worksheet to determine the amount you will need to save each month to achieve your goal.
3. Reevaluate your progress on a regular basis.

Today's Date _____

Financial goal _____
Amount needed _____
When needed _____
Risk tolerance _____

Value of Initial Investment
1. Amount to accumulate _____
2. Amount of initial investment (if any) _____
3. Number of years (n) _____
4. Average after-tax return (i) _____
5. FVIF(n years, i return)
   (from Appendix A-1) _____
6. Future value of initial investment
   (= line 2 × line 5) _____

Regular Investment Payments	Annual	Monthly
7. Amount remaining to meet goal (= Line 1 − Line 6)	_____	_____
8. FVIFA (n periods, i return) (from Appendix A-3)	_____	_____
9. Payment necessary to reach goal (= line 7 ÷ line 8)	_____	_____

WORKSHEET 44 investment risk tolerance

<u>Directions</u>: Select the answer that best represents your opinion:

_____ **1.** Three months after you put money in an investment, the price drops by 25 percent. If nothing else has changed about the company, what would you do?

    a. Sell to avoid further worry and try something else.

    b. Do nothing and wait for the price to go back up again.

    c. Buy more, since it's a cheap investment now and you still like the company.

_____ **2.** Consider the same situation as in question 1, but assume that the investment is part of a portfolio targeted to achieve a short-term objective (three years or less in the future). What would you do?

    a. Sell.

    b. Do nothing.

    c. Buy more.

_____ **3.** Consider the same situation as in question 1, but assume that the investment is part of a portfolio targeted to achieve a long-term objective (15 years or more in the future). What would you do?

    a. Sell.

    b. Do nothing.

    c. Buy more.

_____ **4.** You are investing for retirement, which is at least 40 years in the future. What would you rather do?

    a. Invest in a low-risk money market fund. You know that the returns will be low, but you like having virtually no risk of default or of losing any of your accumulated funds.

    b. Invest half in bonds and half in stocks. The bonds will give you the security of having regular cash flows, and the stocks will allow for some growth in the value of your portfolio.

    c. Invest all in aggressive growth (high-risk, high-return) stock funds. Although the value of your portfolio is likely to go up and down over time, these funds will give you the best chance for large gains. Since you have a long time horizon, you can afford to take a few losses now and then.

_____ **5.** You just won a $10 million lottery. You can either receive an annuity of $400,000 per year for 25 years or a cash lump sum of $4 million. Which would you do?

    a. Take the annuity.

    b. Take the cash, invest it in income-producing securities, and only spend the income.

    c. Take the cash and invest it aggressively.

_____ **6.** You are presented with a great investment opportunity, but you don't have enough cash, so you'll have to borrow to make the investment. Would you take out a loan?

  a. Definitely not.

  b. Maybe.

  c. Yes.

_____ **7.** Which of the following best describes your investment attitudes:

  a. I'm uncomfortable with the idea of my portfolio value fluctuating. I'm willing to give up the possibility of higher returns in order to keep my principal intact. I'm satisfied with an investment that stays ahead of inflation.

  b. I expect the value of my investments to fluctuate, but not too much. I could potentially suffer a loss of 3 to 5 percent in a single year, but I'm willing to accept this risk for the opportunity to earn higher returns.

  c. Increasing the value of my portfolio is my goal. I'm willing to risk an occasional drop of 10 percent or more in my investments for the opportunity to achieve superior growth.

Scoring:

Add up the number of a, b, and c answers you gave and score your risk tolerance as follows:

Number of a answers _____ × 1 = _____

Number of b answers _____ × 2 = _____

Number of c answers _____ × 3 = _____

Total score   _____

If you scored 7 to 12, you may be a conservative investor.

If you scored 13 to 16, you may be a moderate investor.

If you scored 17 to 21, you may be an aggressive investor.

[WORKSHEET 45] matching goals and investments

Directions:

For each of your financial goals, identify the time horizon, the amount needed, and the level of risk you are willing to bear. Based on these factors, identify investment alternatives that would be appropriate to consider.

Financial Goal	Time Horizon	Amount Needed	Acceptable Level of Risk	Investments Appropriate for Time Horizon and Acceptable Level of Risk

	Stock 1	Stock 2	Stock 3	Stock 4	Stock 5	Stock 6	Total Portfolio
Company name							
Industry classification							
Income/growth classification							
Market capitalization							
Annual dividend							
P/E ratio							
Earnings per share							
Purchase price							
Number purchased							
Total initial investment							

Date   **Market Values**

	Bond 1	Bond 2	Bond 3	Bond 4	Bond 5	Bond 6	Total Portfolio
Bond issuer							
Bond rating							
Coupon rate							
Maturity date							
Annual dividend							
Face value per bond							
Number purchased							
Total face value							
YTM (%) (date of purchase							

Date   **Market Values**

[WORKSHEET 48] evaluating mutual fund alternatives

Directions:
Identify an investment objective for which mutual fund investments would be appropriate. Based on your objectives, time horizon, and risk tolerance, identify the fund classification(s) you wish to consider. Evaluate alternative funds by completing this worksheet.

1. Investment Objective _____

2. Appropriate type of fund _____

	Mutual Fund Alternatives		
	A	**B**	**C**
Company name			
Fund objective			
Price per share			
Net asset value			
Minimum initial purchase			
Minimum additional purchase			
Past performance			
1-year			
3-year			
5-year			
Expenses			
Front-end load			
Back-end load			
Expense ratio			
Fund manager tenure			
Services			
Auto deduction			
Auto reinvestment			
Transfer between funds			
IRAs			
Online access			
Ratings			
Agency_____			
Agency_____			

mutual fund tracker

	Mutual Fund 1	Mutual Fund 2	Mutual Fund 3	Mutual Fund 4	Mutual Fund 5	Mutual Fund 6	Total Portfolio
Fund name							
Fund family							
Investment objectives							
Portfolio composition							
Industry or sector							
Net asset value							
Price per share							
Number purchased							
Front-end load paid							
Total initial investment							

Date			Market or Net Asset Values				

[WORKSHEET 50] retirement goals

Directions:

For each of the following retirement goals, indicate its importance to you by checking the appropriate box.

Retirement Goal	Very Important	Somewhat Important	Not At All Important
Economic security			
Maintain standard of living	☐	☐	☐
Improve standard of living	☐	☐	☐
Financial independence	☐	☐	☐
Afford to keep home	☐	☐	☐
Family			
Bequests to heirs	☐	☐	☐
College costs	☐	☐	☐
Support children or parents	☐	☐	☐
Continue family business	☐	☐	☐
Medical			
Cover health-care costs	☐	☐	☐
Extras			
Better/more vacations	☐	☐	☐
Increased hobby costs	☐	☐	☐
Contributions to charity	☐	☐	☐
Other			
_____			
_____			

STEP 1. Estimate before-tax income needs.
    a. Enter current household expenses. _____
    b. Adjust for changes in expenses in retirement.
        Possible reductions: Employment expenses   _____   _____
                               Retirement savings   _____   _____
                               Housing expenses   _____   _____
                    Total reductions   _____
        Possible increases: Health care/insurance   _____
                               Leisure activities   _____
                               Gifts/donations   _____
                    Total increases   _____
    c. Adjusted expenses in current dollars (1a. − 1b. + 1c.) _____
    d. Adjust for inflation to future dollars
    (i = expected inflation; n = years to retirement).
    Aftertax income needs = Adjusted expenses in current dollars $\times (1+i)^n$ = _____
    e. Calculate before-tax total income needs.
        $ Before tax = $ After-tax/(1 − average tax rate)   = _____

STEP 2. Estimate annual retirement income from defined benefit
retirement plan(s).
Use most recent statement from your pension sponsor
or estimate based on known benefit formula.
        Plan 1_____
        Plan 2_____
Total income from defined benefit plans   = _____

STEP 3. Estimate annual retirement income from social security.
Use calculator at www.ssa.gov or Exhibit 15-4 to estimate
in future dollars.   = _____

STEP 4. Calculate retirement income shortfall. (1e − 2 − 3)   = _____

STEP 5. Estimate total retirement wealth needed.
    a. Retirement wealth factor: _____
    (from Exhibit 15-6, assuming ___ years in retirement and
    ___% average investment return)
    b. Retirement income shortfall $\times$ Retirement wealth factor   = _____

STEP 6. Estimate retirement savings goal
    a. Value of current retirement savings accounts   = _____
    b. Future value of current accounts (= 6a $\times FVIF_{i,n}$)   = _____
    c. Retirement savings goal (5b−6b)   = _____

STEP 7. Estimate monthly savings required to meet savings goal.   = _____
(Use time value of money calculation for payment.)

STEP 1. Estimate total college costs:
Use table below to estimate the annual
costs for one year of college.
Total costs = Annual cost × 4   _____ × 4 =   _____

STEP 2. Subtract other sources of funding:
Grants and scholarships
Child's own savings or employment income   _____
Support from other family   _____
Future value of current savings   _____
Total from other sources   _____

STEP 3. College fund needed (Step 1 − Step 2)   _____

STEP 3. Calculate monthly savings needed:
FV = College fund needed (Step 3)   _____
N = Number of periods to save   _____
I = After-tax return per period   _____
Solve for PMT.   _____

Alternative method: PMT $= \dfrac{\text{College fund needed}}{\text{FVIFA}_{i\%,n}}$

Child's Age Today	Public In-State School Annual College Cost Inflation			Public Out-of-State School Annual College Cost Inflation			Private University Annual College Cost Inflation		
	4%	6%	8%	4%	6%	8%	4%	6%	8%
18	$13,500	$13,500	$13,500	$19,500	$19,500	$19,500	$34,000	$34,000	$34,000
17	14,040	14,310	14,580	20,280	20,670	21,060	35,360	36,040	36,720
16	14,602	15,169	15,746	21,091	21,910	22,745	36,774	38,202	39,658
15	15,186	16,079	17,006	21,935	23,225	24,564	38,245	40,495	42,830
14	15,793	17,043	18,367	22,812	24,618	26,530	39,775	42,924	46,257
13	16,425	18,066	19,836	23,725	26,095	28,652	41,366	45,500	49,957
12	17,082	19,150	21,423	24,674	27,661	30,944	43,021	48,230	53,954
11	17,765	20,299	23,137	25,661	29,321	33,420	44,742	51,123	58,270
10	18,476	21,517	24,988	26,687	31,080	36,093	46,531	54,191	62,932
9	19,215	22,808	26,987	27,755	32,945	38,981	48,393	57,442	67,966
8	19,983	24,176	29,145	28,865	34,922	42,099	50,328	60,889	73,403
7	20,783	25,627	31,477	30,019	37,017	45,467	52,341	64,542	79,276
6	21,614	27,165	33,995	31,220	39,238	49,104	54,435	68,415	85,618
5	22,478	28,795	36,715	32,469	41,592	53,033	56,612	72,520	92,467
4	23,378	30,522	39,652	33,768	44,088	57,275	58,877	76,871	99,865
3	24,313	32,354	42,824	35,118	46,733	61,857	61,232	81,483	107,854
2	25,285	34,295	46,250	36,523	49,537	66,806	63,681	86,372	116,482
1	26,297	36,352	49,950	37,984	52,509	72,150	66,229	91,554	125,801
0	27,349	38,534	53,946	39,503	55,660	77,922	68,878	97,048	135,865

WORKSHEET 53 | life Insurance needs analysis

	Yourself	Your Spouse

A. Costs at Death

1. Uninsured medical expenses (deductible and copay) _____ _____
2. Funeral expense (average $10,000, but less for cremation) _____ _____
3. Settlement of estate (estimate 4% of assets) _____ _____
4. State inheritance taxes (if any) _____ _____
5. Counseling costs for adjustment to loss _____ _____

Total costs at death $1 + 2 + 3 + 4 + 5$ _____ _____

B. Lump Sums

6. Outstanding debts
   a. Mortgage _____ _____
   b. Car loan(s) _____ _____
   c. Credit cards and other loans _____ _____
   Total outstanding debt to repay $6a + 6b + 6c$ _____ _____
7. Education costs for children or spouse (see Chapter 15) _____ _____
8. Spouse retirement fund _____ _____
9. Household emergency fund
   Monthly household expenses $\times$ 3 _____ _____

Total lump sum needs $6d + 7 + 8 + 9$ _____ _____

C. Cost of Household Maintenance

10. Deceased annual after-tax income _____ _____
11. Annual cost of lost support services
    (child/eldercare, housekeeping) _____ _____
12. Reduction in family expenses
    due to death (estimated 20–25%) _____ _____
13. Annual Social Security survivor benefits _____ _____
14. Net income shortfall $10 + 11 - 12 - 13$ _____ _____

Total household maintenance fund needs
Line 14 x Number of years to replace _____ years _____ _____

15. **Total fund needed (sum double-underlined values)** _____ _____

D. Available Resources to Meet Needs

16. Total savings and investments _____ _____
17. Group life insurance _____ _____
18. Social Security lump sum benefit _____ _____
19. **Total resources to meet needs** $16 + 17 + 18$ _____ _____

Total life insurance needs $15 - 19$ _____ _____

Directions:

Use the following checklist to help you organize your personal and financial information for estate-planning purposes. Your list should include the location of relevant documents and any necessary contact information. Copies of the list and individual documents should be given to someone you trust for safekeeping.

✓	Estate-Planning Documents	Location
☐	Wills (including living will and letter of last instruction)	
☐	Trust documents	
☐	Powers of attorney (durable power of attorney or health-care power of attorney)	
☐	Tax returns (federal and state income tax, gift tax, and estate tax)	
☐	Personal legal records and identification (birth and marriage certificates, divorce decrees, court judgments, military records, Social Security cards)	
☐	Bank account information (account numbers, address and phone of financial institutions)	
☐	Investment information (brokerage accounts, mutual funds, CDs, annuities, stocks and bonds)	
☐	Debt information (loans and credit cards)	
☐	Business interests (partnership and buy-sell agreements, sole proprietorships)	
☐	Retirement account documents (401(k), Keogh, and other retirement investment accounts, pension plans)	
☐	Social Security records (annual statements, earnings and benefits histories)	
☐	Insurance policies (life, health, and long-term care)	
☐	Real estate and personal property (deeds, mortgages, title insurance, rental property records, time-shares, vehicle titles, leases)	

WORKSHEET 55   **estate tax calculation**

1. Calculate gross estate:
    Net worth   _____
    Less assets excluded because of
    type of ownership or beneficiary
    designation:
    Assets transferred through family limited partnerships   _____
    Life insurance held in irrevocable trusts   _____
    Other irrevocable trust assets   _____
  Gross estate   _____

2. Calculate adjusted gross estate
    Funeral expenses   _____
    Executor's fee   _____
    Legal fees   _____
    Court fees   _____
    Estate administration fees   _____
    Total estate expenses   _____
    Adjusted gross estate = Gross estate − Estate expenses   _____

3. Calculate taxable estate
    Amount to spouse   _____
    Amount to charity   _____
    Total unlimited deductions   _____
  Taxable estate = Adjusted gross estate − Unlimited deductions   _____

4. Unified exemption ($1.5 million in 2005)   _____
    Amount subject to tax = Taxable estate − Exemption   _____

[APPENDIX A] time value of money calculations

EXHIBIT A-1 Future Value of a Lump Sum ($FVIF_{i\%,n}$)

$$FV = PV \times (1+i)^n$$
$$= PV \times FVIF_{i,n}$$

EXHIBIT A-2 Present Value of a Lump Sum ($PVIF_{i\%,n}$)

$$PV = FV \times \left(\frac{1}{1+i}\right)^n$$

$$= FV \times PVIF_{i,n}$$

EXHIBIT A-3 Future Value of an Annuity ($FVIFA_{i\%,n}$)

$$FVA = PMT \times \frac{(1+i)^n - 1}{i}$$

$$= PMT \times FVIFA_{i,n}$$

EXHIBIT A-4 Present Value of an Annuity ($PVIFA_{i\%,n}$)

$$PVA = PMT \times \frac{1 - \left(\frac{1}{1+i}\right)^n}{i}$$

$$= PMT \times PVIFA_{i,n}$$

EXHIBIT A-5 Monthly Payment Factors

$$PMT = \frac{\text{Loan Amount}}{1,000} \times \text{Payment factor}_{i,n}$$

EXHIBIT A-6 Present Value of Monthly Payments (Mortgage factor$_{i\%,n}$)

Maximum mortgage amount = Affordable mortgage payment $\times$ Mortgage factor$_{i,n}$

APPENDIX A — time value of money calculations

Exhibit A-1 Future Value of a Lump Sum of $1 Compounded for a Given Number of Periods (FVIF$_{i,n}$)

Periods	1%	2%	3%	4%	5%	6%	7%	8%	9%	10%	11%
1	1.010	1.020	1.030	1.040	1.050	1.060	1.070	1.080	1.090	1.100	1.110
2	1.020	1.040	1.061	1.082	1.103	1.124	1.145	1.166	1.188	1.210	1.232
3	1.030	1.061	1.093	1.125	1.158	1.191	1.225	1.260	1.295	1.331	1.368
4	1.041	1.082	1.126	1.170	1.216	1.262	1.311	1.360	1.412	1.464	1.518
5	1.051	1.104	1.159	1.217	1.276	1.338	1.403	1.469	1.539	1.611	1.685
6	1.062	1.126	1.194	1.265	1.340	1.419	1.501	1.587	1.677	1.772	1.870
7	1.072	1.149	1.230	1.316	1.407	1.504	1.606	1.714	1.828	1.949	2.076
8	1.083	1.172	1.267	1.369	1.477	1.594	1.718	1.851	1.993	2.144	2.305
9	1.094	1.195	1.305	1.423	1.551	1.689	1.838	1.999	2.172	2.358	2.558
10	1.105	1.219	1.344	1.480	1.629	1.791	1.967	2.159	2.367	2.594	2.839
11	1.116	1.243	1.384	1.539	1.710	1.898	2.105	2.332	2.580	2.853	3.152
12	1.127	1.268	1.426	1.601	1.796	2.012	2.252	2.518	2.813	3.138	3.498
13	1.138	1.294	1.469	1.665	1.886	2.133	2.410	2.720	3.066	3.452	3.883
14	1.149	1.319	1.513	1.732	1.980	2.261	2.579	2.937	3.342	3.797	4.310
15	1.161	1.346	1.558	1.801	2.079	2.397	2.759	3.172	3.642	4.177	4.785
16	1.173	1.373	1.605	1.873	2.183	2.540	2.952	3.426	3.970	4.595	5.311
17	1.184	1.400	1.653	1.948	2.292	2.693	3.159	3.700	4.328	5.054	5.895
18	1.196	1.428	1.702	2.026	2.407	2.854	3.380	3.996	4.717	5.560	6.544
19	1.208	1.457	1.754	2.107	2.527	3.026	3.617	4.316	5.142	6.116	7.263
20	1.220	1.486	1.806	2.191	2.653	3.207	3.870	4.661	5.604	6.727	8.062
25	1.282	1.641	2.094	2.666	3.386	4.292	5.427	6.848	8.623	10.835	13.585
30	1.348	1.811	2.427	3.243	4.322	5.743	7.612	10.063	13.268	17.449	22.892
35	1.417	2.000	2.814	3.946	5.516	7.686	10.677	14.785	20.414	28.102	38.575
40	1.489	2.208	3.262	4.801	7.040	10.286	14.974	21.725	31.409	45.259	65.001
45	1.565	2.438	3.782	5.841	8.985	13.765	21.002	31.920	48.327	72.890	109.530
50	1.645	2.692	4.384	7.107	11.467	18.420	29.457	46.902	74.358	117.391	184.565

Periods	12%	13%	14%	15%	16%	17%	18%	19%	20%	25%	30%
1	1.120	1.130	1.140	1.150	1.160	1.170	1.180	1.190	1.200	1.250	1.300
2	1.254	1.277	1.300	1.323	1.346	1.369	1.392	1.416	1.440	1.563	1.690
3	1.405	1.443	1.482	1.521	1.561	1.602	1.643	1.685	1.728	1.953	2.197
4	1.574	1.630	1.689	1.749	1.811	1.874	1.939	2.005	2.074	2.441	2.856
5	1.762	1.842	1.925	2.011	2.100	2.192	2.288	2.386	2.488	3.052	3.713
6	1.974	2.082	2.195	2.313	2.436	2.565	2.700	2.840	2.986	3.815	4.827
7	2.211	2.353	2.502	2.660	2.826	3.001	3.185	3.379	3.583	4.768	6.275
8	2.476	2.658	2.853	3.059	3.278	3.511	3.759	4.021	4.300	5.960	8.157
9	2.773	3.004	3.252	3.518	3.803	4.108	4.435	4.785	5.160	7.451	10.604
10	3.106	3.395	3.707	4.046	4.411	4.807	5.234	5.695	6.192	9.313	13.786
11	3.479	3.836	4.226	4.652	5.117	5.624	6.176	6.777	7.430	11.642	17.922
12	3.896	4.335	4.818	5.350	5.936	6.580	7.288	8.064	8.916	14.552	23.298
13	4.363	4.898	5.492	6.153	6.886	7.699	8.599	9.596	10.699	18.190	30.288
14	4.887	5.535	6.261	7.076	7.988	9.007	10.147	11.420	12.839	22.737	39.374
15	5.474	6.254	7.138	8.137	9.266	10.539	11.974	13.590	15.407	28.422	51.186
16	6.130	7.067	8.137	9.358	10.748	12.330	14.129	16.172	18.488	35.527	66.542
17	6.866	7.986	9.276	10.761	12.468	14.426	16.672	19.244	22.186	44.409	86.504
18	7.690	9.024	10.575	12.375	14.463	16.879	19.673	22.901	26.623	55.511	112.455
19	8.613	10.197	12.056	14.232	16.777	19.748	23.214	27.252	31.948	69.389	146.192
20	9.646	11.523	13.743	16.367	19.461	23.106	27.393	32.429	38.338	86.736	190.050
25	17.000	21.231	26.462	32.919	40.874	50.658	62.669	77.388	95.396	264.698	705.641
30	29.960	39.116	50.950	66.212	85.850	111.065	143.371	184.675	237.376	807.794	2,619.996
35	52.800	72.069	98.100	133.176	180.314	243.503	327.997	440.701	590.668	2,465.190	9,727.860
40	93.051	132.782	188.884	267.864	378.721	533.869	750.378	1,051.668	1,469.772	7,523.164	36,118.865
45	163.988	244.641	363.679	538.769	795.444	1,170.479	1,716.684	2,509.651	3,657.262	22,958.874	134,106.817
50	289.002	450.736	700.233	1,083.657	1,670.704	2,566.215	3,927.357	5,988.914	9,100.438	70,064.923	497,929.223

[APPENDIX A] time value of money calculations

Exhibit A-2 Present Value of a Lump Sum of $1 to Be Received at the End of a Given Number of Periods (PVIF$_{i,n}$)

Periods	1%	2%	3%	4%	5%	6%	7%	8%	9%	10%	11%
1	0.990	0.980	0.971	0.962	0.952	0.943	0.935	0.926	0.917	0.909	0.901
2	0.980	0.961	0.943	0.925	0.907	0.890	0.873	0.857	0.842	0.826	0.812
3	0.971	0.942	0.915	0.889	0.864	0.840	0.816	0.794	0.772	0.751	0.731
4	0.961	0.924	0.888	0.855	0.823	0.792	0.763	0.735	0.708	0.683	0.659
5	0.951	0.906	0.863	0.822	0.784	0.747	0.713	0.681	0.650	0.621	0.593
6	0.942	0.888	0.837	0.790	0.746	0.705	0.666	0.630	0.596	0.564	0.535
7	0.933	0.871	0.813	0.760	0.711	0.665	0.623	0.583	0.547	0.513	0.482
8	0.923	0.853	0.789	0.731	0.677	0.627	0.582	0.540	0.502	0.467	0.434
9	0.914	0.837	0.766	0.703	0.645	0.592	0.544	0.500	0.460	0.424	0.391
10	0.905	0.820	0.744	0.676	0.614	0.558	0.508	0.463	0.422	0.386	0.352
11	0.896	0.804	0.722	0.650	0.585	0.527	0.475	0.429	0.388	0.350	0.317
12	0.887	0.788	0.701	0.625	0.557	0.497	0.444	0.397	0.356	0.319	0.286
13	0.879	0.773	0.681	0.601	0.530	0.469	0.415	0.368	0.326	0.290	0.258
14	0.870	0.758	0.661	0.577	0.505	0.442	0.388	0.340	0.299	0.263	0.232
15	0.861	0.743	0.642	0.555	0.481	0.417	0.362	0.315	0.275	0.239	0.209
16	0.853	0.728	0.623	0.534	0.458	0.394	0.339	0.292	0.252	0.218	0.188
17	0.844	0.714	0.605	0.513	0.436	0.371	0.317	0.270	0.231	0.198	0.170
18	0.836	0.700	0.587	0.494	0.416	0.350	0.296	0.250	0.212	0.180	0.153
19	0.828	0.686	0.570	0.475	0.396	0.331	0.277	0.232	0.194	0.164	0.138
20	0.820	0.673	0.554	0.456	0.377	0.312	0.258	0.215	0.178	0.149	0.124
25	0.780	0.610	0.478	0.375	0.295	0.233	0.184	0.146	0.116	0.092	0.074
30	0.742	0.552	0.412	0.308	0.231	0.174	0.131	0.099	0.075	0.057	0.044
35	0.706	0.500	0.355	0.253	0.181	0.130	0.094	0.068	0.049	0.036	0.026
40	0.672	0.453	0.307	0.208	0.142	0.097	0.067	0.046	0.032	0.022	0.015
45	0.639	0.410	0.264	0.171	0.111	0.073	0.048	0.031	0.021	0.014	0.009
50	0.608	0.372	0.228	0.141	0.087	0.054	0.034	0.021	0.013	0.009	0.005

Periods	12%	13%	14%	15%	16%	17%	18%	19%	20%	25%	30%
1	0.893	0.885	0.877	0.870	0.862	0.855	0.847	0.840	0.833	0.800	0.769
2	0.797	0.783	0.769	0.756	0.743	0.731	0.718	0.706	0.694	0.640	0.592
3	0.712	0.693	0.675	0.658	0.641	0.624	0.609	0.593	0.579	0.512	0.455
4	0.636	0.613	0.592	0.572	0.552	0.534	0.516	0.499	0.482	0.410	0.350
5	0.567	0.543	0.519	0.497	0.476	0.456	0.437	0.419	0.402	0.328	0.269
6	0.507	0.480	0.456	0.432	0.410	0.390	0.370	0.352	0.335	0.262	0.207
7	0.452	0.425	0.400	0.376	0.354	0.333	0.314	0.296	0.279	0.210	0.159
8	0.404	0.376	0.351	0.327	0.305	0.285	0.266	0.249	0.233	0.168	0.123
9	0.361	0.333	0.308	0.284	0.263	0.243	0.225	0.209	0.194	0.134	0.094
10	0.322	0.295	0.270	0.247	0.227	0.208	0.191	0.176	0.162	0.107	0.073
11	0.287	0.261	0.237	0.215	0.195	0.178	0.162	0.148	0.135	0.086	0.056
12	0.257	0.231	0.208	0.187	0.168	0.152	0.137	0.124	0.112	0.069	0.043
13	0.229	0.204	0.182	0.163	0.145	0.130	0.116	0.104	0.093	0.055	0.033
14	0.205	0.181	0.160	0.141	0.125	0.111	0.099	0.088	0.078	0.044	0.025
15	0.183	0.160	0.140	0.123	0.108	0.095	0.084	0.074	0.065	0.035	0.020
16	0.163	0.141	0.123	0.107	0.093	0.081	0.071	0.062	0.054	0.028	0.015
17	0.146	0.125	0.108	0.093	0.080	0.069	0.060	0.052	0.045	0.023	0.012
18	0.130	0.111	0.095	0.081	0.069	0.059	0.051	0.044	0.038	0.018	0.009
19	0.116	0.098	0.083	0.070	0.060	0.051	0.043	0.037	0.031	0.014	0.007
20	0.104	0.087	0.073	0.061	0.051	0.043	0.037	0.031	0.026	0.012	0.005
25	0.059	0.047	0.038	0.030	0.024	0.020	0.016	0.013	0.010	0.004	0.001
30	0.033	0.026	0.020	0.015	0.012	0.009	0.007	0.005	0.004	0.001	0.0004
35	0.019	0.014	0.010	0.008	0.006	0.004	0.003	0.002	0.002	0.0004	0.0001
40	0.011	0.008	0.005	0.004	0.003	0.002	0.001	0.001	0.0007	0.0001	0.00003
45	0.006	0.004	0.003	0.002	0.001	0.001	0.001	0.0004	0.0003	0.00004	0.00001
50	0.003	0.002	0.001	0.001	0.001	0.0004	0.0003	0.0002	0.0001	0.00001	0.000002

Exhibit A-3 Future Value of a Given Number of $1 End-of-Period Payments (FVIFA$_{i,n}$)

Periods	1%	2%	3%	4%	5%	6%	7%	8%	9%	10%	11%
1	1.000	1.000	1.000	1.000	1.000	1.000	1.000	1.000	1.000	1.000	1.000
2	2.010	2.020	2.030	2.040	2.050	2.060	2.070	2.080	2.090	2.100	2.110
3	3.030	3.060	3.091	3.122	3.153	3.184	3.215	3.246	3.278	3.310	3.342
4	4.060	4.122	4.184	4.246	4.310	4.375	4.440	4.506	4.573	4.641	4.710
5	5.101	5.204	5.309	5.416	5.526	5.637	5.751	5.867	5.985	6.105	6.228
6	6.152	6.308	6.468	6.633	6.802	6.975	7.153	7.336	7.523	7.716	7.913
7	7.214	7.434	7.662	7.898	8.142	8.394	8.654	8.923	9.200	9.487	9.783
8	8.286	8.583	8.892	9.214	9.549	9.897	10.260	10.637	11.028	11.436	11.859
9	9.369	9.755	10.159	10.583	11.027	11.491	11.978	12.488	13.021	13.579	14.164
10	10.462	10.950	11.464	12.006	12.578	13.181	13.816	14.487	15.193	15.937	16.722
11	11.567	12.169	12.808	13.486	14.207	14.972	15.784	16.645	17.560	18.531	19.561
12	12.683	13.412	14.192	15.026	15.917	16.870	17.888	18.977	20.141	21.384	22.713
13	13.809	14.680	15.618	16.627	17.713	18.882	20.141	21.495	22.953	24.523	26.212
14	14.947	15.974	17.086	18.292	19.599	21.015	22.550	24.215	26.019	27.975	30.095
15	16.097	17.293	18.599	20.024	21.579	23.276	25.129	27.152	29.361	31.772	34.405
16	17.258	18.639	20.157	21.825	23.657	25.673	27.888	30.324	33.003	35.950	39.190
17	18.430	20.012	21.762	23.698	25.840	28.213	30.840	33.750	36.974	40.545	44.501
18	19.615	21.412	23.414	25.645	28.132	30.906	33.999	37.450	41.301	45.599	50.396
19	20.811	22.841	25.117	27.671	30.539	33.760	37.379	41.446	46.018	51.159	56.939
20	22.019	24.297	26.870	29.778	33.066	36.786	40.995	45.762	51.160	57.275	64.203
25	28.243	32.030	36.459	41.646	47.727	54.865	63.249	73.106	84.701	98.347	114.413
30	34.785	40.568	47.575	56.085	66.439	79.058	94.461	113.283	136.308	164.494	199.021
35	41.660	49.994	60.462	73.652	90.320	111.435	138.237	172.317	215.711	271.024	341.590
40	48.886	60.402	75.401	95.026	120.800	154.762	199.635	259.057	337.882	442.593	581.826
45	56.481	71.893	92.720	121.029	159.700	212.744	285.749	386.506	525.859	718.905	986.639
50	64.463	84.579	112.797	152.667	209.348	290.336	406.529	573.770	815.084	1,163.909	1,668.771

Periods	12%	13%	14%	15%	16%	17%	18%	19%	20%	25%	30%
1	1.000	1.000	1.000	1.000	1.000	1.000	1.000	1.000	1.000	1.000	1.000
2	2.120	2.130	2.140	2.150	2.160	2.170	2.180	2.190	2.200	2.250	2.300
3	3.374	3.407	3.440	3.473	3.506	3.539	3.572	3.606	3.640	3.813	3.990
4	4.779	4.850	4.921	4.993	5.066	5.141	5.215	5.291	5.368	5.766	6.187
5	6.353	6.480	6.610	6.742	6.877	7.014	7.154	7.297	7.442	8.207	9.043
6	8.115	8.323	8.536	8.754	8.977	9.207	9.442	9.683	9.930	11.259	12.756
7	10.089	10.405	10.730	11.067	11.414	11.772	12.142	12.523	12.916	15.073	17.583
8	12.300	12.757	13.233	13.727	14.240	14.773	15.327	15.902	16.499	19.842	23.858
9	14.776	15.416	16.085	16.786	17.519	18.285	19.086	19.923	20.799	25.802	32.015
10	17.549	18.420	19.337	20.304	21.321	22.393	23.521	24.709	25.959	33.253	42.619
11	20.655	21.814	23.045	24.349	25.733	27.200	28.755	30.404	32.150	42.566	56.405
12	24.133	25.650	27.271	29.002	30.850	32.824	34.931	37.180	39.581	54.208	74.327
13	28.029	29.985	32.089	34.352	36.786	39.404	42.219	45.244	48.497	68.760	97.625
14	32.393	34.883	37.581	40.505	43.672	47.103	50.818	54.841	59.196	86.949	127.913
15	37.280	40.417	43.842	47.580	51.660	56.110	60.965	66.261	72.035	109.687	167.286
16	42.753	46.672	50.980	55.717	60.925	66.649	72.939	79.850	87.442	138.109	218.472
17	48.884	53.739	59.118	65.075	71.673	78.979	87.068	96.022	105.931	173.636	285.014
18	55.750	61.725	68.394	75.836	84.141	93.406	103.740	115.266	128.117	218.045	371.518
19	63.440	70.749	78.969	88.212	98.603	110.285	123.414	138.166	154.740	273.556	483.973
20	72.052	80.947	91.025	102.444	115.380	130.033	146.628	165.418	186.688	342.945	630.165
25	133.334	155.620	181.871	212.793	249.214	292.105	342.603	402.042	471.981	1,054.791	2,348.803
30	241.333	293.199	356.787	434.745	530.312	647.439	790.948	966.712	1,181.882	3,227.174	8,729.985
35	431.663	546.681	693.573	881.170	1,120.713	1,426.491	1,816.652	2,314.214	2,948.341	9,856.761	32,422.868
40	767.091	1,013.704	1,342.025	1,779.090	2,360.757	3,134.522	4,163.213	5,529.829	7,343.858	30,088.655	120,392.883
45	1,358.230	1,874.165	2,590.565	3,585.128	4,965.274	6,879.291	9,531.577	13,203.424	18,281.310	91,831.496	447,019.389
50	2,400.018	3,459.507	4,994.521	7,217.716	10,435.649	15,089.502	21,813.094	31,515.336	45,497.191	280,255.693	1,659,760.743

[APPENDIX A] time value of money calculations

Exhibit A-4 Present Value of a Given Number of $1 End-of-Period Payments (PVIFA $_{i,n}$)

Periods	1%	2%	3%	4%	5%	6%	7%	8%	9%	10%	11%
1	0.990	0.980	0.971	0.962	0.952	0.943	0.935	0.926	0.917	0.909	0.901
2	1.970	1.942	1.913	1.886	1.859	1.833	1.808	1.783	1.759	1.736	1.713
3	2.941	2.884	2.829	2.775	2.723	2.673	2.624	2.577	2.531	2.487	2.444
4	3.902	3.808	3.717	3.630	3.546	3.465	3.387	3.312	3.240	3.170	3.102
5	4.853	4.713	4.580	4.452	4.329	4.212	4.100	3.993	3.890	3.791	3.696
6	5.795	5.601	5.417	5.242	5.076	4.917	4.767	4.623	4.486	4.355	4.231
7	6.728	6.472	6.230	6.002	5.786	5.582	5.389	5.206	5.033	4.868	4.712
8	7.652	7.325	7.020	6.733	6.463	6.210	5.971	5.747	5.535	5.335	5.146
9	8.566	8.162	7.786	7.435	7.108	6.802	6.515	6.247	5.995	5.759	5.537
10	9.471	8.983	8.530	8.111	7.722	7.360	7.024	6.710	6.418	6.145	5.889
11	10.368	9.787	9.253	8.760	8.306	7.887	7.499	7.139	6.805	6.495	6.207
12	11.255	10.575	9.954	9.385	8.863	8.384	7.943	7.536	7.161	6.814	6.492
13	12.134	11.348	10.635	9.986	9.394	8.853	8.358	7.904	7.487	7.103	6.750
14	13.004	12.106	11.296	10.563	9.899	9.295	8.745	8.244	7.786	7.367	6.982
15	13.865	12.849	11.938	11.118	10.380	9.712	9.108	8.559	8.061	7.606	7.191
16	14.718	13.578	12.561	11.652	10.838	10.106	9.447	8.851	8.313	7.824	7.379
17	15.562	14.292	13.166	12.166	11.274	10.477	9.763	9.122	8.544	8.022	7.549
18	16.398	14.992	13.754	12.659	11.690	10.828	10.059	9.372	8.756	8.201	7.702
19	17.226	15.678	14.324	13.134	12.085	11.158	10.336	9.604	8.950	8.365	7.839
20	18.046	16.351	14.877	13.590	12.462	11.470	10.594	9.818	9.129	8.514	7.963
25	22.023	19.523	17.413	15.622	14.094	12.783	11.654	10.675	9.823	9.077	8.422
30	25.808	22.396	19.600	17.292	15.372	13.765	12.409	11.258	10.274	9.427	8.694
35	29.409	24.999	21.487	18.665	16.374	14.498	12.948	11.655	10.567	9.644	8.855
40	32.835	27.355	23.115	19.793	17.159	15.046	13.332	11.925	10.757	9.779	8.951
45	36.095	29.490	24.519	20.720	17.774	15.456	13.606	12.108	10.881	9.863	9.008
50	39.196	31.424	25.730	21.482	18.256	15.762	13.801	12.233	10.962	9.915	9.042

Periods	12%	13%	14%	15%	16%	17%	18%	19%	20%	25%	30%
1	0.893	0.885	0.877	0.870	0.862	0.855	0.847	0.840	0.833	0.800	0.769
2	1.690	1.668	1.647	1.626	1.605	1.585	1.566	1.547	1.528	1.440	1.361
3	2.402	2.361	2.322	2.283	2.246	2.210	2.174	2.140	2.106	1.952	1.816
4	3.037	2.974	2.914	2.855	2.798	2.743	2.690	2.639	2.589	2.362	2.166
5	3.605	3.517	3.433	3.352	3.274	3.199	3.127	3.058	2.991	2.689	2.436
6	4.111	3.998	3.889	3.784	3.685	3.589	3.498	3.410	3.326	2.951	2.643
7	4.564	4.423	4.288	4.160	4.039	3.922	3.812	3.706	3.605	3.161	2.802
8	4.968	4.799	4.639	4.487	4.344	4.207	4.078	3.954	3.837	3.329	2.925
9	5.328	5.132	4.946	4.772	4.607	4.451	4.303	4.163	4.031	3.463	3.019
10	5.650	5.426	5.216	5.019	4.833	4.659	4.494	4.339	4.192	3.571	3.092
11	5.938	5.687	5.453	5.234	5.029	4.836	4.656	4.486	4.327	3.656	3.147
12	6.194	5.918	5.660	5.421	5.197	4.988	4.793	4.611	4.439	3.725	3.190
13	6.424	6.122	5.842	5.583	5.342	5.118	4.910	4.715	4.533	3.780	3.223
14	6.628	6.302	6.002	5.724	5.468	5.229	5.008	4.802	4.611	3.824	3.249
15	6.811	6.462	6.142	5.847	5.575	5.324	5.092	4.876	4.675	3.859	3.268
16	6.974	6.604	6.265	5.954	5.668	5.405	5.162	4.938	4.730	3.887	3.283
17	7.120	6.729	6.373	6.047	5.749	5.475	5.222	4.990	4.775	3.910	3.295
18	7.250	6.840	6.467	6.128	5.818	5.534	5.273	5.033	4.812	3.928	3.304
19	7.366	6.938	6.550	6.198	5.877	5.584	5.316	5.070	4.843	3.942	3.311
20	7.469	7.025	6.623	6.259	5.929	5.628	5.353	5.101	4.870	3.954	3.316
25	7.843	7.330	6.873	6.464	6.097	5.766	5.467	5.195	4.948	3.985	3.329
30	8.055	7.496	7.003	6.566	6.177	5.829	5.517	5.235	4.979	3.995	3.332
35	8.176	7.586	7.070	6.617	6.215	5.858	5.539	5.251	4.992	3.998	3.333
40	8.244	7.634	7.105	6.642	6.233	5.871	5.548	5.258	4.997	3.999	3.333
45	8.283	7.661	7.123	6.654	6.242	5.877	5.552	5.261	4.999	4.000	3.333
50	8.304	7.675	7.133	6.661	6.246	5.880	5.554	5.262	4.999	4.000	3.333